THE BONES BELOW

BY SIERRA DeMULDER

A Write Bloody Book
Long Beach. CA USA

The Bones Below
by Sierra DeMulder

Write Bloody Publishing ©2010.
1ˢᵗ printing.
Printed in USA

The Bones Below Copyright 2010.
All Rights Reserved.

Published by Write Bloody Publishing.

Printed in Long Beach, CA USA.

Cover Designed by Joshua Grieve
Interior Layout by Lea C. Deschenes
Edited by Derrick Brown, shea M gauer, Saadia Byram, Michael Sarnowski
Proofread by Sarah Kay
Type set in Helvetica Neue and Bell MT

To contact the author, send an email to writebloody@gmail.com

WRITE BLOODY PUBLISHING
LONG BEACH, CA

THE BONES BELOW

For Brian & my sisters

"And then the day came, when the risk to remain tight in a bud was more painful than the risk it took to Blossom."

—Anaïs Nin

AT FIRST SIGHT

When she stops kissing you
with her mouth open,
find the screw driver.

Buy a newly cut shank of beef.
Leave so much blood in the kitchen
she has to ask what happened.

When she no longer calls you *baby*,
hide all the silverware
between the couch cushions.

Send her there to sleep.
If she does not complain,
let the sinks in the bathroom overflow.

Bake the wedding photos
in the dryer. Stand in
the middle of your flood.

Call her name backwards, forwards.
Wave your arms like your chest is a runway.
She is the plane you are crashing.

When she does not reach
for you, pretend
it is the first time

you've met.

MISPLACING THEIR RING FINGERS

The summer my parents lost their marriage
like so many magnets kicked under the refrigerator,
my cousin and I named trees after babysitters
we never had. We lived in our bathing suits,
washed our hair in pond water and sunburned.

(Once, my mother slammed the screen
door so hard, I comforted the hinges.) I taught
my cousin how to make face paint out of spit
and dirt. She taught me to swim underwater.

(Once, I found my father weeping on the bed
they did not share anymore.) On the green carpet
of summer, we played until the cicadas, dressed
in dusk, called us to dinner. We kissed goodnight
and I ran home barefoot in the dark.

(Once, I sat between my parents and placed their hands
in my lap like a seatbelt. I do not remember this.)
To this day, walking at night on that creaking road
still reminds me of wolves.

FOR MY EXES

1
on the little league
field we traded virginities
like baseball cards.

2 & 3
I do not regret
leaving you, but there are things
we still don't speak of.

4a
still masturbate while
thinking about you. feel used
in an empty room.

4b
the first day we met,
I told you I missed you
already. I still do.

5
you kissed me so hard
my lips bruised. I still look for
you in the mirror.

6
If I wrote you a
love poem, it would smell like
ash. I burned many.

SILT

in this town, you don't buy new
things before October, not until after
the back-to-school clothing has gone on sale.

you only shower twice a week, go to school
when you have to, when you can't find a dollar
in your mother's purse to spend at the arcade.

you go to parties where the sweating necks
of beer bottles stumble through corn fields.
a handle of cheap vodka, a lip swollen with chew.

here, you don't go to college.
at home, your father speaks only to the wallpaper,
tells it what debt feels like soaked in bourbon.

you tack pictures of naked women
and 12-point bucks above your pillow.
you dream of floods.

SOME LIKE IT HOT

"Hollywood's a place where
they'll pay you a thousand dollars for kiss,
and fifty cents for your soul."
—Marilyn Monroe

It took the embalmer three days to prepare your body.

He removed a half moon of flesh from the base
of your hairline; sutured it as tight as your corset
to reduce the postmortem swelling of your pretty little neck.
Those infamous breasts deflated as a result of the autopsy.
Under your favorite chartreuse dress, you were stuffed
like a doll with scraps of cotton.

Marilyn, you were our first wet dream, our first taste of sweat.
Your lips pursed like two virgins shivering in anticipation.
We knew you were a good kisser just by looking at you –
the kind of woman who made wives dig their nails
into the forearms of their husbands.

When did you start believing you looked better in photographs?

You were found naked in bed, clutching a telephone,
flat-line dial tone singing you to sleep.
We all pretended you were trying to call us.

O, ECONOMY
(PART 1)

Today, I plan on stealing from the grocery store
and washing my laundry by hand in the bathtub.

DURING THE MONTH IT TOOK YOU TO LEAVE ME:

I filled my gas tank to 33 dollars and 33 cents
and told you it was for you
because it was your favorite number.

I organized our belongings
(white t-shirts—books—toothbrushes—
baby, this is where we keep our sweaters)
as if using the word "our" would embed myself
into what you call home.

I bought flowers from a homeless man
because you are a botany major.
I wanted to bring them to you,
wilting and loveless, and show you how
I can nurture something worth saving.

There is a five-finger scar above my breast.
There is an orchestra on my neck shaped like your pulse
from all the nights you held me the way
you only hold something slipping.

There are 6 states
pressed like stubborn flowers
between the last time I kissed you and today,
but you still feel like a sound caught in my throat.

PAPER DOLLS

We are taught
from the moment we leave our pink nurseries
we are collapsible paper dolls:
light to hold, easier to crumple.
That as women, our worth lives secretly
wrapped in lace and cotton panties,
our fragility armored in pepper spray and mace.

They say one in three women will be raped
or sexually abused in their lifetime.
I am one of three daughters.

Imagine each victim is an acrobat.
Her sanity, a balancing act.
Our response is the unfailing safety net.
We never expect to see her across the wire.

You weren't just violated, we tell her,
you are an empty museum, a gutted monument
to what used to hold so much worth.
With best intentions we tell her to reclaim it,
put a price tag on her rape and own it.
Don't stand too tall, don't act too strong.
We will name you *denial.*
Come back when you are ready to crumble
like your bones are made of chalk.

You can only laugh cutely or cry beautifully,
so cry beautifully.
We will catch you.

We are calling it theft,
as if he could pluck open your ribs like cello strings,
pocket your breasts, steal what makes your heart flutter
and tack its wings to his wall.

Some days you will feel dirty.
Some weeks you'll remember how hard it is to breathe in public,
but know this:

the person who did this to you is broken. Not you.
The person who did this to you is out there,
choking on the glass of his chest.
It is a windshield
and his heartbeat is a baseball bat:
regret this, regret this.

Nothing was stolen from you.
Your body is not a hand-me-down.
There is nothing that sits inside you holding your worth,
no locket that can be seen or touched,
fucked from your stomach to be left on concrete.

I know it's hard to feel perfect
when you can't tell an Adam's apple from a fist.
Some ashtray of a man picked you to play his Eden
but I will not watch you collapse.

WHAT TO DO AFTER YOU'VE MEMORIZED THE FACE OF THE PERSON YOU LOVE

Find the smallest pore on their cheek and name it.

Count how many eyelashes go missing at the end of the day and mourn.

Measure precisely how many kisses it takes to get from elbow to wrist.

Study their knees, meticulously.

TO RESENT THE WRAPPING PAPER

The way
children wait for presents,
your mother was anxious for you.

I caught her looking for you
under the bed,
behind the door,
wrapped on the top shelf of the closet.

A week past your due date,
I found her pacing the hallways,
rubbing her belly like a swollen lamp.

It's a complicated anger
to be jealous of your own skin.

2/2/08

Today is your birthday.
I wish you would answer my calls
so I could tell you how much
I ~~wish you were never born~~
miss you.

UNDER APRON

Peach tea does not
make eye contact and asks
to steep the bag himself.
I slide the package across the counter—
no contact necessary.
Another orders
an Americano, room for cream
with a sticky accent, tells me how
her children are doing in school.
Medium skim latte watches
suspiciously as I draw the shots.
I know the names of some,
remember most by their order.
Single espresso.
Small soy chai.
Large cappuccino.

Some must think I do not
have the parts to hear them
hiss across the counter.
Perhaps they forget how
we are made of the same thing—mistake
the espresso grind for my voice.
My hair only mops.

COME. SIT. HEEL. STAY.

When I took your virginity,
I did it carelessly, like a dog
left alone in a butcher shop.
I taught you the way adults love
(quick, dry, no eye contact.)

A year later, in the back of your car,
you showed me what you had learned,
what kind of man I had trained you to be.

There was nothing playful
in the way you hit, tenderizing meat.
Scraping at skin as if you were trying
to take back what you lost inside of me.

By the time you came on my back,
my nipples were chapped
and gnawed as bones. My legs raw,
newly butchered lambs.

MRS. DAHMER

I caught you once,
killing a squirrel in our backyard with a rock.
Your 8-year-old body shivering, illuminated.
Through tears, you told me you loved it.
I assumed you meant the squirrel.

Even after I watched the news—
clips of a 10-gallon blue vat being carried out of your building,
your refrigerator sealed with police tape,
pictures of the boys you kissed too hard.
Even after I heard what they found in your refrigerator,
(two human heads and a heart in your freezer)
I could not bring myself to call you a monster.

Your father told the reporters
when I was pregnant with you, I experienced seizure-like fits,
foaming at the mouth. My swollen body would stiffen
and my eyes would peel back like paint
as if I was trying to look at you.

The day your apartment building was gutted and paved over,
I began to obsess over your baby pictures, looking for anything
that could predict the way you learned to love seeing
     things inside out.

Your brother legally changed his last name
but I cannot erase the stretch marks. I still see your eyes in
    my mirror.
The scar where they pulled you like Persephone from my stomach.

There is no reminiscing here.
No one wants to hear how you were a wonderful child,
they only want to watch your car crash of a life on repeat.
Your adolescent obsession with road kill—
how you would bike for miles with a garbage bag
filled with whatever cadavers you found on the street.
How could I possibly not see this coming, they say.

Did I hold you too tightly when we crossed the street?
Child, when your father and I fought at night, did you
    mistake it for lovemaking?
Did I teach those fingers to pluck families apart like flower petals?
(I love you, I love you still.)
Darling, was it the sound of the dead dog's bones, as your father
dropped them one by one into the bucket that seduced you?
Did it sound too much like your pulse?
Was it the day I drove away from you—
freshly graduated from high school,
2 months premature of your first murder.
Did I put too many states between us?
Did you put your own heart in the freezer
next to the thought of me?

Would Mary be forsaken if Jesus had not grown
to be the son God had intended to father?
If he did not wear a crown of thorns,
but instead, wrapped it around his knuckles?
Will I be forgiven for the sins I did not commit,
but created?

When you were small, I told you:
you can grow up to be anything.

WHAT WE HIDE FROM OTHERS

you followed me into the bathroom
where I drunkenly pulled down my pants
and sat on the toilet. you stood at the sink
and commented on my underwear,
not looking long enough to notice the scars
on my thighs. you have never seen me naked
but this does not stop you from calling me
lover. after I flushed, we snorted cocaine
out of a parliament filter and stared
side by side into the mirror, matching
flared nostrils, renovated hearts,
blood down the front of our shirts.

ONE A.M.

*"The destruction of the world is the last,
almost desperate attempt to save myself
from being crushed by it."*
—Erich Fromm

she is the kind of shaken
that makes me feel perfect—
pale and empty like the frames of barns
about to be torn down.

the girl isn't old.
she bleeds green sapling branches,
ignorant to how cold the winter will be.
lonely in silence, she makes
every blinking eyelash
a collision.

the first day we met,
she kissed me
drunk on wine and gasoline.
I couldn't taste it then,
but her chest is a hallway.

don't give her matches;
she will kiss them.
don't give her sweat;
she will drink it.

left alone, she will shatter your teacups
and ash on your love seats,
sit shotgun as you drive on her guilt.
she will hang up, stare dirty, laugh crazy.

she will wake you,
steal you away from dreams of leaves,
holding her forearm like a paintbrush as the blood
splatters solar systems on our kitchen tile.
she will laugh like the bottom of vodka bottles.
apologize for overshooting 11 stitches.

I wish I was the one with the needle and thread.
I would hem her hands over themselves
so she would know how it felt to be helpless.

HEART APNEA

When he sleeps,
the snoring does not bother me:
the rhythmic growl, gravel shoveled
across the sidewalk of his throat.

It is the grasping, desperate way
in which he takes in air – his gulping lungs
as if every dream is filled with water
and he is trying to inflate
the life jacket under his skin.

I babble in my sleep. He believes
I am trying to tell him how my heart works,
says he will translate the manual one day.
I want to ask him: *am I the ocean?*
Are you drowning in everything
I don't say when I'm awake?

DISTRACTION

The television whines like an ignored
child in the corner of their living room.
Arguments stop mid-insult only to mouth
along to their favorite jingles. They fight

like handfuls of broken silverware, hurling
the name of their 9-month-old distraction
as a knife: *this is your problem.*

When the baby begins to talk, I wonder
if he will sound like sitcom laughter.
Will he respond only to Regret? His first
words, "I'm sorry."

O, ECONOMY
(PART 2)

Things I am planning to sell on Craigslist:

blender
book shelf
toothbrush (used)
mint condition textbooks
gym membership
vintage lamp he bought for me on Craigslist
the still-wrapped Christmas present I bought for my sister
a road map
my stuffed panda I puked on when I was 6
an antique chest I found on the street after the flood
the sewing machine my mother taught me to use
the quilt that she made for me with it
the promise I made him
a microwave
heart (used)
27 hangers
this poem
a nice table from IKEA

WHEN THE APOCALYPSE COMES

and all the windows are shattered
and the car tires have melted into the pavement,
once all of the schools and hospitals
and skyscrapers have folded in on themselves
and the last street lamp has wilted like a starving flower,

I will still want to fuck you.

We both know I can't handle stress well.
I'm anxious, claustrophobic, and things between us
haven't always been easy—you nitpick, I'm stubborn,
and we have been fighting
over pointless things
like directions,
how you never take me anywhere nice anymore.
I saw the way you smiled at that poet
and her pomegranate metaphors SUCKED.

But sweetheart,
when a meteor crashes through
our kitchen ceiling, I will not panic.
When the locusts envelop the neighborhood
and our shower water thickens to blood,
I promise not to bite my nails.

I won't even get angry when you don't answer your phone—
even as the pavement begins to crack and spew like a rotten egg,
you will not get 47 missed phone calls in 4 minutes
(even though we both know it's possible).

When the news anchor finally tell us the truth—
that there is no hope—I won't even think about
joining the angry mob outside
our burning apartment building.
Baby, no.

I will put on my least flammable negligee
and I will find you.

I will crawl to you across this curdling parking lot of a city,
lick your body new again like my tongue
is God's hand trying to erase and recreate the earth.
For 6 days straight, we will be
what makes the sidewalk blister.

Day 1: in the beginning,
I will find you, pull you into me.

Day 2: we will make the earth
and the sky jealous.

Day 3: I want you to fuck me
bent over a crumpled taxi.

4: in the graveyard of a strip mall.

5: on the steps of the capitol,
in every store, on every mattress that isn't on fire.
This world is a melting candle
we're only using for foreplay.

Day 6: You may think I'm in denial,
that I am avoiding the bigger issue here
but you didn't even look at me
the last time you said *I love you*

and, shit, if it didn't feel like the end of the world.

I know this can't be healthy
(pretending everything is on fire), but baby,
we could be the most beautiful wreckage
in all this smoke.

When the apocalypse does come,
I will rebuild our city with my tongue.
I will suck this world's ashes from your fingers.
I will refuse to let the fires of this hell
be the only thing that makes us sweat.

When the apocalypse comes,
so will we.

I CRASHED YOUR CAR
For Rya

While you were in Japan,
(teaching English to children)
I crashed your car.

It made a horrible crunching sound, so loud
I was sure you must have heard it
from halfway around the world.

That's why I waited so long to tell you.

THE OTHER WOMAN

I pretend I don't love it
when you hold my hand in public,
when you catch a wild hair in the net of your fingers,
when you kiss me right in front of the gas station cashier.

I remember we live in a big city.
I secretly imagine the scandal we could cause
if we lived in a small town, where everyone knew your name
and your bed: how our love would spill like paint cans
across old wooden porches. It would seep
between the cracks of the floorboards,
the way I live beneath your fingernails
when you go home to her.

STATIC

Somehow, there is silence.
People are running, their mute eyes panicking
like deer who have never seen the oncoming glare
of judgment. A single red flower blooms in the center of her shirt.
She finally looks at you.

Rewind 1 week: she sits in front of you in science and
    smells like ice cream.
You wonder if she even knows your name—wonder if she
    would ever notice your thimble
of existence. To them you are nothing but the skinned
    knees of the student body.
They will read about you, (the ones who are lucky,
who will see death and not meet it) how you walked like a god
unnoticed among them, planned a revolution for your fingers
to pluck pulses like arrows from bows.

Rewind 1 week: a sharpie in the boys' bathroom screams
    hollow point prophecies.
It goes unnoticed. You go unnoticed in the hallways,
    stepped over like broken glass.
You count how many people make eye contact and don't make it
to your second hand.

Rewind 1 week: The whole world is sleeping.
You are wrapped in a straight jacket of alarm clocks and
    school bells;
the only one conscious in a city built of zombies.

Rewind 1 week: the guidance counselor asks if there is
    trouble at home.
"You never speak in class, you eat lunch alone" but how
could he possibly relate to this Armageddon in your head,
to the static collecting between your knuckles.
You stare at the picture of his perfect framed family,
imagine each of them crying. You tell him and his photograph
to go to hell.

Fast-forward 4 weeks:
this is hell.
3 bodies down,
6, 7.

Rewind 8 days: you wonder if heaven exists
or if it's just a Santa Claus lie to make you sleep at night
and be nice to others.

Fast-forward 7 days: she catches you staring.
Calls you a freak. You forget what is like to feel anything but fire.
The hallways laugh. The lockers punch back.

Fast-forward 1 day: you drag the weapon from your belt.
The hallways stop laughing. Their wax smiles start melting.

The sound of gunshots does not scare you, the satisfaction does.
You count shells in your head, fallen bodies out loud.
This is their alarm clock.
This is natural selection.
This is survival.

You rewind. The trigger pushes your finger forward.
The bullet comes spiraling back into the mouth of its barrel.
A single red flower wilts in the center of her shirt.
She finally looks at you.

FIVE YEARS AFTER

You wonder why I don't
answer your 3 a.m. phone calls.

When you say "I miss you,"
I begin to undress myself out of habit.

MASQUERADE

Her skin glows
with impeccable craft
like genetically
altered fruit.
Ten blank canvases of acrylic
stuck awkwardly
to the tips of her fingers.
So much concealer
blankets her face
it is impossible to remember
the color of her eyes,
the natural curl of her brow.
I will never be so
well set, like a dining room table
beautifully disguised
as a feast.

ODE TO CARBONATION

you taste like what I imagine
swallowing radio wires
feels like: all sparks and pop
music in my throat.

ALL THAT BLINDS US

1

You take off your shirt
and all of a sudden,
I have never seen a naked body before.
I stare as if you could be eclipsed
at any moment. I look away,
everything becomes white.

2

You can't bring yourself to look at me.
My shoulders burn like a shadow
is trying to peel itself off.
I am the sidewalk crack,
a black cat, the superstition
of a good woman.

TALKING TO GOD

It's hard these days not to listen,
not to crack eggshells and wait for symphonies,
snap tree branches into splintering answers.

My hips don't feel so heavy these days.
They've gotten used to carrying excuses why
I don't believe in God.
I just talk to him like I do:

hey, where are you?
I've been scared lately
it's still awful dark down here with the lights on
and my eyelashes are making shadows
that look like monsters in the closet
where are you?

My windpipe feels like it echoes these days,
Lately, I've been talking more to myself
than familiar faces. My journal has become
an answering machine for the thoughts I pass on the street
and God is just one of them that's too long of a message
to leave before the beep:

hey,
I thought I saw you today
in the carpet of my sister's apartment
the sun was enfolding itself around you

right before you started to make love to the dust particles,
I tried to find something to hold you in
I missed it
where are you?

what do you look like?
I thought I saw you today
in the soft spot on my niece's head
you didn't look like a man and I didn't see a woman
I just saw divinity so I pressed my ear to her forehead
and listened

But my hands are bonier these days,
dried like papyrus, calloused from gripping
onto theories like heaven isn't a place—it's a feeling.
I still think children are molded from mud.
They age like sun rays and dry like clay.

God, it's not that I don't believe
I feel hardened these days

we are taught too young here
how to point two fingers and cock our thumb
we are worth the sum of our pockets and our verses
divided by the distance between what's crucial and commercial
half of us are broke
the other half is breaking

tell me it's not my fault

split my glazed plaster
into a thousand pieces of appreciation
tell me that you are an artist
you have to be

remind me life is suffering
existence is coincidence
and I am just a witness of half of it

tell me that when we met
it was love at first sight
and that you have a crush on me

Yes, that's right; God has a crush on me.
That's why he is too embarrassed to talk,
he's afraid he might say the wrong thing.

Well I'm listening,
and I'm waiting.
Nobody is an atheist in a foxhole.
This isn't Hell—this isn't even close—
It's hard these days to keep praying
to someone who's got you on hold
when all I want is something to hold on to.

I'm just supposed to know that you're there

So I'll keep eavesdropping on
season uprisings where I think you're hiding,
look for you in the smell of acoustic cedar and cigarettes,
reach deeper into my pockets when I'm looking for a light,
and trust that you're caught somewhere
between my breath tonight.

MEMORIAL

The bonfire
from last night
had been swallowed
by the earth
and covered with white ash.
We placed lawn chairs
on its grave,
sat on the blanket of dust
and spoke about things
we pretended not to miss—
oblivious to the stubborn
kindling that refused
to let go of the fire
which had *burned* so strongly
for it once.

SAWDUST

Above my bed
hangs a dream catcher
braided by my father.

I don't know how,
because his hands are sewn from thick leather—
nimble with a buck knife and hammer
but do not seem gentle enough to twist a spider's web so delicate
it captures his daughter's nightmares.

My father is a hunter and a carpenter.
My childhood memories are of gutted carcasses
hung like wind chimes and venison cut into butterfly wings;
the smell of sawdust is comforting.

When I was little,
we used to hike up the mountain behind our house,
both dressed in matching long johns.
My middle name is Fawn: completely his idea.
I would run behind like his deer
for fear of getting lost without him.

Arrowheads are buried beneath his tilled skin.
Spirits of old medicine men
sleep between the cracks of his eyes.
The antlers mounted on his wall
are hands reaching like a cradle,

spiked, but I know they are smooth—
they feel like handfuls of wind.

One day, he will leave me.
He says he wants to be taken by a heart attack;
a swift grip, no waiting. I imagine his death—how I wish
to see him float on easy like a shaman
rising from his bed, ignoring his arthritic floorboards.
He will wake me gently.

I imagine it will be cold and early.
The grass beneath our feet will still be sleeping.
I will guide his wrist and elbow like a bow and arrow,
up the mountain behind our house; his life painted
in cold smoke exhales like the breath
shared between peace pipes.

He smells like coffee and baby powder.
Blue marble eyes and wheat field blonde hair.
The morning he dies,
the field will be laced with white flowers.
His bones will be light as eagles.

When he is ready,
we will stop, turn, face
the glow of day, breaking dust and dirt apart
like the sun is just opening her eyes.

My father will whisper dandelion seeds into the air.
I will see him run barefoot through small-town streets,
trapping muskrats between his fingers.

I will see him learn like whiplash
what alcohol and being a man tastes like.
His breath will quicken now.
I will remind him that regret does not exist
when you are a mountain – the dirt
does not repent for its shifting,
it merely holds the roots tighter.

As he begins to drift in and out of light,
I will layer him in moss and wool.
As the leaves begin to murmur his pulse
and the trees around us bend in celebration,
I will tell my father that I love him,
that it is okay, and that I won't
get lost on the walk home.

TAXIDERMY

Five years after you daughter's death,
your still cry in the juniors section
of department stores.

You preserve her bedroom like a taxidermist.
Her unworn prom dress still hangs
like a skinned mermaid in her closet.

Cancer entered your home like a greedy tenant,
posed himself into family portraits,
slept in your daughter's bed,
swallowed all her blood cells.

Once, when she was in the other room,
her blood being read like tea leaves,
the doctor suggested not to bother
with college applications.

You couldn't bring yourself to tell her.
You couldn't bring yourself to say it.
Sometimes you think she knew,
as she methodically filled out
each question and box,
it was *never* for her.

There is still a stack of unsent applications
hidden like tumor in your dresser.
She kissed every envelope goodbye.
You couldn't bear to send more of her away.

When she passed,
quietly like a note to God,
all you wanted was to swaddle her
in your arms like an infant, bring her home
from the hospital, fragile and new.
Breastfeed her back to life,
potty train and finger paint,
re-teach her the alphabet,
retrace her first steps
back to you.

To lose a child is like giving birth in reverse.
It is slow and it rips, planting a permanent lump
in your throat.

When chemotherapy pulled out
the last of her hair, you started carrying
her baby teeth in your pocket: A reminder
things can grow back.

THE DOG'S MEDICINE

He baits the pill, wraps it
in expensive cheeses.

Sometimes, she is stubborn
like an ungreased door hinge.

He curls her neck between
his shoulder and forearm,

their bodies adjoined
like a clasp of a necklace.

He pushes the pill
down the inside of her jaw.

I hear it click against
each tooth, like a child

running a stick along
the legs of a fence.

She huffs and struggles
and drools, her mouth filled

with what she doesn't know
is good for her, yet.

When it is swallowed,
his hands are shaking.

Her inability to protest,
the bitch just can't say no.

TO THE WOMAN HITTING ON MY BOYFRIEND:

Do you know
how many people
I kill in my poems?

What about the word *commitment*
do you not understand – Too many letters?
Not enough pictures? Was it not on the cover
of I'm a Dumb Witch Magazine?
(Now I'm a feminist so I avoid
using the B-word in spirit of sisterhood.
But sister, just because I'm a feminist
does not mean I won't cut a bitch.)

You are not discrete.
There is nothing subtle
about pulling my boyfriend aside
to confess your moral dilemma
TO BLOW or NOT TO BLOW.
Ask me, what light through
yonder window breaks?
It will be your fucking face.

I'm sorry;
I'm probably going too far.
You are only flirting.
Let me retract my nails.

Let go of your ponytail
to ask you
as a woman
do not do this.

I trust my lover far more
than you trust your pheromones
but you are temptation after a fight.
You are one more drink at the bar.
You are the uncomfortable silence in the car ride home.
You are a crowbar between us in bed,
my doubt when he hands are open
but his eyes are closed.
You are cold feet tripping down the aisle.
You are standing on the alter licking his earlobe.
You are lipstick stains,
hidden receipts,
flowers that don't know my name.
You are the love poem he wrote for me.

Please,
relationships are hard enough.
People are so fucked up these days.

Dating is like finding the least rusted bear trap
around the ankles of someone
you just might be able to look at
for the rest of your life.

Intimacy is the art of licking wounds.
It's taken me years to let anyone kiss me
when my lips were chapped.

WHEN THE JOHN LOVES THE PROSTITUTE

The way she moves,
as if everything in this town
could pay for a steak.

When she walks,
the streetlights turn upside down;
their pockets shook for change.

She is always pacing,
no matter how much I pay her.
As she undresses, her body uncorks
like a champagne bottle.

This time, I brought her
chocolate-covered cherries.
She does not stay.

RECYCLING

While digging through piles
of tired clothing at the Goodwill
on University Avenue, somewhere
between the broken cassette tapes
and pit-stained blouses, I lost
the last thing he gave me.

It was a birthday gift
from Berlin: a wallet made
from recycled milk cartons.
I frantically searched the aisles
I had just so patiently excavated.

My eyes craved to see it's white corners
hidden under a winter hat or foolishly
laying at the foot of the shoe rack.

I looked for an hour, cried in the car
as if we had celebrated my birthday together,
as if he hadn't left a long time ago,
before any of this clothing was worn.

THE DEATH OF FARRAH FAWCETT

(I pretend you never lost your hair.
Your skin remained the color of peaches.
The sunrise of your mouth never cracked,
your thighs unsoiled; your breasts still swell
and crash like the tide won't let go
of your stomach. I don't want to picture you
bleached and lifeless as sand. But, if I must
imagine you in death,)

You are a white dress
pinned to a clothesline—
dancing uncontrollably,
so bright it hurts
our eyes.

CYCLE OF ABUSE

When your father threw
the dining room chair,
it felt as if the wallpaper flinched.

Maybe it was instinctual.
Hung family portraits
watched your mother for years
sag like an old coat at the sound
of the slamming door.

I never saw him hit her
but in our two-year relationship,
I helped clean up three broken chairs,
four pictures frames, sixteen dishes.

People say, when you marry someone,
you marry their family.

We were barely sixteen, unripe fruit
not ready to be picked, peeled.
I loved you head over handles
like my first bicycle accident –
before the mouthful of gravel and blood,
I swore we were flying.

You were so many firsts:
first boyfriend,
first hand holding mine in the hallways,
first three-hour phone call,
first time to pick a boy over my friends,
first person to see me naked,
bare and fresh as a plate of clay,
first river of fingers,
first fistful of hair,
first time to pick a boy over my family,
first time my body was a scale,
you had so much weight.

Do you remember the drive in?
Your sister in the front seat asks you
to quit shaking your leg without looking back.
I am dry. Your fingers are fish out of water,
flopping and desperate.
You do not stop.

You never hit me
but in our two-year relationship,
you took so much of me in your mouth.
Foreplay was an argument with the ceiling fan.
Your father's voice vibrating up the stairs
Compromise was turning off the lights.
Your mother sitting in silence, my legs
tacked destinations on your map.

Do you remember
the school dance? Outside the cafeteria,
I am pinned like a corsage.
Pressed against the lockers
as if you were the traffic
I am about to run into.
You shake me; tell me
you love me so damn hard.

People say, when you marry someone,
you marry their family.
                    Was that your father
fingering me on couch in front of your siblings?
Was he the one who made you ignore the no's,
to slide them under the pillow with your hands?
Were they his hands, making the wallpaper
of my skin flinch? Is this where
the cycle of abuse found you,
as the picture frames looked away.

I still worry about your mother,
imagine her crumpled like a rag on the floor,
a handful of shattered china, her silence
a familiar taste in my throat.

JOURNAL ENTRY

My life is slowing slipping into summer. I have worn the same tank top for 4 days in a row, I take lukewarm showers; I sweat behind my knees and between my elbows.

Today, it is 90 degrees and the winds are up to 45 miles per hour. It feels like the ocean is everywhere in Minnesota.

ACKNOWLEDGEMENTS

I wish to thank the people who have shown me so much love and encouragement. You have taught me how to be honest and how to feel beautiful. In no particular order, all of my heart is divided between Cheyenne, Rya, Mom, Dad, Michael, Khary, Colin, Derrick, Brian, and Sam, each and every member of the Intangibles, my friends and the family of poets that continues to grow. I love you.

The poems "Mrs. Dahmer" and "Distraction" appeared previously in *Lamplighter Review.*

ABOUT THE AUTHOR

Sierra DeMulder is a Pushcart-nominated performance poet, touring and competing at venues across the country. In 2009 alone, she won the National Poetry Slam Championship, was awarded Best Female Poet at College Union Poetry Slam Invitational, and ranked 9th at the Individual World Poetry Slam. Sierra is a member of the Intangible Spoken Word Collective. She has been trying not to trip since 1986.

NEW FROM WRITE BLOODY BOOKS

EVERYTHING IS EVERYTHING (2010)
New poems by Cristin O'Keefe Aptowicz

DEAR FUTURE BOYFRIEND (2010)
A Write Bloody reissue of Cristin O'Keefe Aptowicz's first book of poetry

HOT TEEN SLUT (2010)
A Write Bloody reissue of Cristin O'Keefe Aptowicz's second book of poetry about her time writing for porn

WORKING CLASS REPRESENT (2010)
A Write Bloody reissue of Cristin O'Keefe Aptowicz's third book of poetry

OH, TERRIBLE YOUTH (2010)
A Write Bloody reissue of Cristin O'Keefe Aptowicz's fourth book of poetry about her terrible youth

CATACOMB CONFETTI (2010)
New poems by Josh Boyd

THE BONES BELOW (2010)
New poems by Sierra DeMulder

CEREMONY FOR THE CHOKING GHOST (2010)
New poems by Karen Finneyfrock

MILES OF HALLELUJAH (2010)
New poems by Rob "Ratpack Slim" Sturma

RACING HUMMINGBIRDS (2010)
New poems by Jeanann Verlee

YOU BELONG EVERYWHERE (2010)
Road memoir and how-to guide for travelling artists

LEARN THEN BURN (2010)
Anthology of poems for the classroom. Edited by Tim Stafford and Derrick Brown.

OTHER WRITE BLOODY BOOKS

STEVE ABEE, GREAT BALLS OF FLOWERS (2009)
New poems by Steve Abee

SCANDALABRA (2009)
New poetry compilation by Derrick Brown

DON'T SMELL THE FLOSS (2009)
New Short Fiction Pieces By Matty Byloos

THE LAST TIME AS WE ARE (2009)
New poems by Taylor Mali

ANIMAL BALLISTICS (2009)
New poems by Sarah Morgan

CAST YOUR EYES LIKE RIVERSTONES INTO THE EXQUISITE DARK (2009)
New poems by Danny Sherrard

SPIKING THE SUCKER PUNCH (2009)
New poems by Robbie Q. Telfer

THE GOOD THINGS ABOUT AMERICA (2009)
An illustrated, un-cynical look at our American Landscape. Various authors.
Edited by Kevin Staniec and Derrick Brown

THE ELEPHANT ENGINE HIGH DIVE REVIVAL (2009)
Anthology

THE CONSTANT VELOCITY OF TRAINS (2008)
New poems by Lea C. Deschenes

HEAVY LEAD BIRDSONG (2008)
New poems by Ryler Dustin

UNCONTROLLED EXPERIMENTS IN FREEDOM (2008)
New poems by Brian Ellis

POLE DANCING TO GOSPEL HYMNS (2008)
Poems by Andrea Gibson

CITY OF INSOMNIA (2008)
New poems by Victor D. Infante

WHAT IT IS, WHAT IT IS (2008)
Graphic Art Prose Concept book by Maust of Cold War Kids and author Paul Maziar

OVER THE ANVIL WE STRETCH (2008)
New poems by Anis Mojgani

IN SEARCH OF MIDNIGHT: THE MIKE MCGEE HANDBOOK OF AWESOME (2009)
New poems by Mike McGee

NO MORE POEMS ABOUT THE MOON (2008)
NON-Moon poems by Michael Roberts

WRITE BLOODY ANTHOLOGIES

JUNKYARD GHOST REVIVAL (2008)
with Andrea Gibson, Buddy Wakefield, Anis Mojgani, Derrick Brown, Robbie Q,
Sonya Renee and Cristin O'Keefe Aptowicz

THE LAST AMERICAN VALENTINE:
ILLUSTRATED POEMS TO SEDUCE AND DESTROY (2008)
24 authors, 12 illustrators team up for a collection of non-sappy love poetry.
Edited by Derrick Brown

LETTING MYSELF GO (2007)
Bizarre god comedy & wild prose by Buzzy Enniss

LIVE FOR A LIVING (2007)
New poems by Buddy Wakefield

SOLOMON SPARROWS ELECTRIC WHALE REVIVAL (2007)
Poetry compilation by Buddy Wakefield, Anis Mojgani, Derrick Brown, Dan
Leamen & Mike McGee

I LOVE YOU IS BACK (2006)
Poetry compilation (2004-2006) by Derrick Brown

BORN IN THE YEAR OF THE BUTTERFLY KNIFE (2004)
Poetry anthology, 1994-2004 by Derrick Brown

SOME THEY CAN'T CONTAIN (2004)
Classic poetry compilation by Buddy Wakefield

WWW.WRITEBLOODY.COM

WRITEBLOODY
QUALITY AMERICAN BOOKS

PULL YOUR BOOKS UP BY THEIR BOOTSTRAPS

Write Bloody Publishing distributes and promotes great books of fiction, poetry and art every year. We are an independent press dedicated to quality literature and book design, with an office in Long Beach, CA.

Our employees are authors and artists so we call ourselves a family. Our design team comes from all over America: modern painters, photographers and rock album designers create book covers we're proud to be judged by.

We publish and promote 8-12 tour-savvy authors per year. We are grass-roots, D.I.Y., bootstrap believers. Pull up a good book and join the family. Support independent authors, artists and presses.

Visit us online:
writebloody.com

LaVergne, TN USA
23 April 2010
180307LV00001B/10/P